*E*ach and every day, you are on
the way to becoming the person
you were meant to be. Every day
brings you closer to reaching your
potential, your hopes, and your
wishes on a thousand stars. Each
day gives you a new opportunity to
be the miracle that you are.

— Douglas Pagels

# 7 DAYS TO A POSITIVE ATTITUDE

## A One-Week Game Plan for Beginning the Journey Toward Brighter Days

A Blue Mountain Arts® Collection

Edited by Gary Morris

**Blue Mountain Press**™

Boulder, Colorado

Library of Congress Catalog Card Number: 2004013254
ISBN: 0-88396-860-6

ACKNOWLEDGMENTS appear on page 80.

Certain trademarks are used under license.
BLUE MOUNTAIN PRESS is registered in U.S. Patent and Trademark Office.

Printed in the United States of America.
First Printing: 2004

 This book is printed on recycled paper.

This book is printed on fine quality, laid embossed, 80 lb. paper. This paper has been specially produced to be acid free (neutral pH) and contains no groundwood or unbleached pulp. It conforms with all the requirements of the American National Standards Institute, Inc., so as to ensure that this book will last and be enjoyed by future generations.

**Library of Congress Cataloging-in-Publication Data**

7 days to a positive attitude : a one-week game plan for beginning the journey toward brighter days / edited by Gary Morris.
p. cm.
"A Blue Mountain Arts collection."
ISBN 0-88396-860-6 (soft cover : alk. paper)
1. Attitude (Psychology) 2. Change (Psychology) 3. Optimism. I. Title: Seven days to a positive attitude. II. Morris, Gary, 1958-

BF327.S48 2004
158.1—dc22

2004013254
CIP

# Blue Mountain Arts, Inc.
P.O. Box 4549, Boulder, Colorado 80306

# Contents

# Introduction

Obviously, this book can't guarantee that one week from today your life will be completely transformed. But it does offer the inspiring message that by taking small daily steps you can ultimately achieve profound, long-term, and lasting changes. It's a game plan, in a way, of a possible path you can take toward achieving a more positive outlook. You can visualize where you want to be in the future and make peace with your past; build a support group full of optimistic people; learn from setbacks and failures; create a powerful confidence that overcomes mistakes — and rarely procrastinates; and take time to relax and enjoy this golden moment you're living in.

If you can take just one week out of your life and live it with all the optimism, confidence, and hope you can muster... you may find yourself liking it so much you'll never want to look back. Maybe you'll rediscover what means the most to you and decide to pursue it with renewed intensity. Maybe you'll unlock something within you that has been waiting a lifetime to be expressed. Maybe you'll even decide that where you are right now is just perfect for you — but you'll see it through new eyes and appreciate it in deeper ways.

As you go through the week, believe that all you seek to achieve really is possible. Hold tenaciously to your inner confidence. Celebrate your progress and the little victories along the way; learn from the negative moments and disappointments; rely on all the resources available to you. Most of all, remember that every day you are on your way to a brighter, more positive world!

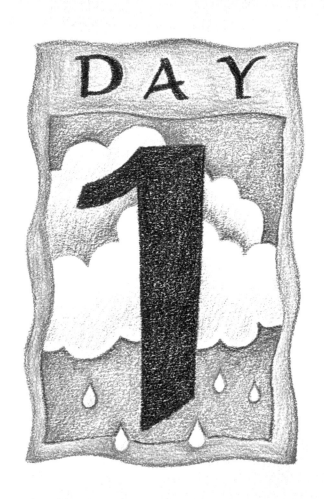

# "Visualize the Perfect Week..."

*You are today where your thoughts have brought you;*
*you will be tomorrow where your thoughts take you.*

James Allen

One of the best ways to create a more optimistic spirit is to have a strong, sure sense of where your life is going. When you commit yourself to a positive plan of action, you focus on the destination and don't get so bogged down over daily obstacles. Today, ask yourself: "Where would I like to be one week from now?" If the next seven days could go exactly as you wish, how would you spend them? Would you start something new — or finish a project that's been neglected far too long? What would your attitude be toward your job, your friends and loved ones, the direction of your dreams?

Make today the first stage on your journey to a brighter future. Set some time aside and imagine what changes you'd like to make. Write down anything that fills you with a sense of potential, enthusiasm, and hope. (See page 11 for some guidelines on setting up your list.) Lay out specific steps you can take to achieve your goals. Prioritize them, break them down into their key components, anticipate any situations and people you may encounter, and make a game plan for dealing with them in a confident manner that advances you in the directions you choose.

Above all, as you dream about and plan for what lies ahead, remember that you are your own best guide to doing what's right for your life. Trust your instincts, listen to your heart... and get set for a great, life-transforming week!

# Plan Your Progress

*He who every morning plans the transaction of the day and follows out that plan, carries a thread that will guide him through the maze of the most busy life. But where no plan is laid, where the disposal of time is surrendered merely to the chance of incidence, chaos will soon reign.*

— Victor Hugo

Tremendous things are accomplished when you take the time to plan. If you're procrastinating because you don't know where to start, try creating a detailed framework of what you need to do, whom you need to contact, and what materials you need in order to begin. When you break down big jobs into a series of smaller steps, something that looked impossible can suddenly seem manageable and achievable. If you're stuck somewhere along the way, your plan can help you get back on track or give you the insight you need to change your approach or your direction.

Take some time today and make a list of where you'd like to go this week. By writing down your goals, you bring them from the realm of thought into the world of action — and thereby set in motion the forces of the universe that will help you make your dreams come true.

# Steps to Great and Productive "List-Making":

- ***Start with the big picture.*** *Whether it's losing weight, finding a new job, or improving your relationships, choose the situations in your life you feel most passionate about changing. Enthusiasm and motivation are the engines of transformation.*

- ***Break it down into specific steps.*** *Instead of saying "I'll get in shape," commit yourself to exercising fifteen minutes a day. Mark it on your calendar and check it off. As you write down precise details of your plan, it's easier to visualize it coming true.*

- ***Don't overdo it.*** *Remember, this list is for one week only! Sticking to a few very specific goals enables you to concentrate all your efforts on them; it also makes it harder to find excuses for not acting.*

- ***Be sure to include rewards.*** *Small rewards are a great way to mark your progress and also motivate yourself to keep with the program.*

- ***Be prepared for setbacks along the way.*** *Life is full of daily distractions that you can't always prepare for. If you don't fulfill a daily goal, don't belittle yourself; just get back on track tomorrow.*

- ***Check your list daily — whenever you think you need some positive reinforcement.*** *Stay focused and strong and remember you're going to accomplish everything one day at a time.*

# Be Prepared; Be Committed

*The moment one definitely commits oneself, then providence moves, too. All sorts of things occur to help one that would never otherwise have occurred. A whole stream of events issues from the decision, raising in one's favor all manner of unforeseen incidents and meetings and material assistance, which no man could have dreamed would have come his way.*

— Johann Wolfgang von Goethe

*Seek out that particular mental attribute which makes you feel most deeply and vitally alive, along with which comes the inner voice which says, "This is the real me," and when you have found that attitude, follow it.*

—William James

# Be Ready to Change Your Life

*We are haunted by an ideal life, and it is because we have within us the beginning and the possibility of it.*

— Phillips Brooks

*Changes are often for the best. They can be difficult to deal with at first, but changes can lead to new possibilities and positive things that you'll only discover once you let go of the past.*

*When a new beginning unfolds in the story of your life, wonderful things can come into view... Brand-new mornings can beckon you. New promises can be made. New commitments can be kept. New ways of seeing the world can make you wonder why you never envisioned this before. New people can care. New smiles can appear. New memories can be made. Old worries can fade and make you wonder why they even bothered you so much to begin with.*

*Today is a gift that can't wait to be unwrapped and to show you what's inside.*

— Douglas Pagels

# In the Week Ahead...
# Be the Person
# You Are Meant to Be

Don't ever be afraid to be who you are. Don't keep yourself from expressing love, kindness, and patience. Don't cut yourself off from the things that nourish your soul. Live in the spirit of life; there are no walls to keep you captive. You are as beautiful as you choose to be.

Take a step you have not dared to take before — a leap of faith, a stride in a new direction. Discover a new creation within yourself. When you think you have reached an end, watch for life to take a turn and renew itself.

*Remember that irritations often produce a pearl; your shortcomings become your strengths. May you find yourself to be like a seed when springtime comes, and grow in your own season.*

*Do not try to change who you are; change the way you look at things. Expand your viewpoint. Be aware of the new directions that open every minute. Like a conductor, you can direct a chorus of many circumstances to create a harmonious life. Assume responsibility for whatever life sends your way. Be victorious in the way you respond to everything that happens to you. Live on the great ocean of possibilities, and sail away toward your dreams.*

— Tanya P. Shubin

# "Today Is Your
# New Beginning..."

*Every morning is a fresh beginning. Every day is the world made
new. Today is a new day. Today is my world made new. I have
lived all my life up to this moment, to come to this day. This
moment — this day — is as good as any moment in all eternity.
I shall make of this day — each moment of this day —
a heaven on earth. This is my day of opportunity.*

Dan Custer

Today is your opportunity to begin a new week with a more
optimistic attitude. You can break away from the past and look
forward to a future that will fulfill you in new, positive ways.

Yet this is also the day when the good intentions and hopes you
dreamed about yesterday will meet the reality of your world as
it is. Chances are, the rest of the world hasn't spent any time
thinking about how to make life easier for you! Your plans and
goals will be tested in ways you never imagined — from the
negative situations and people you encounter to your own
thoughts and behavior patterns that may block your progress.

As you go through this day, the most important thing you can
focus on is your own inner state of being. While you may not
control events or people around you, you are absolutely in
charge of how you respond to them. Making a conscious effort
to react in positive ways, no matter how difficult it may be, has
the power to change your environment in remarkable ways.
Today especially, remember: *The choice is in your hands.* Do all
you can to make this day a strong beginning to the week ahead.

# Get on the Fast Track
# to a Positive Attitude

*We cannot choose how many years we will live, but we can choose how much life those years will have. We cannot control the beauty of our face, but we can control the expression on it. We cannot control life's difficult moments, but we can choose to make life less difficult. We cannot control the negative atmosphere of the world, but we can control the atmosphere of our minds. Too often we try to choose and control things we cannot. Too seldom we choose to control what we can... our attitude.*

— Author Unknown

*The positive thinker has a longer and more penetrative insight. He is completely objective. He has definitive goals. He never takes no for an answer... He just keeps on fighting and thinking and praying and working, and you'd be surprised how many times the positive thinker comes out of the toughest and seemingly most hopeless situations with positive results.*

— Norman Vincent Peale

*As you begin changing your thinking, start immediately to change your behavior. Begin to act the part of the person you would like to become. Take action on the behavior you admire by making it your behavior. Too many people want to feel, then take action. This never works.*

— John C. Maxwell

# Give Your Confidence a Boost

You can increase your feeling of confidence within a few minutes, even within a few seconds — all you have to do is accomplish something that brings you one step closer to one of your goals, and your confidence will instantly grow. The moment you take even the first step of action towards achieving a dream, your sense of confidence will begin expanding, because you'll trust that you can count on yourself. The more steps you take, the better you'll feel about yourself because you are DOING, and that new confidence will help you create even better results.

— Barbara De Angelis

The way to develop self-confidence is to do the thing you fear and get a record of successful experiences behind you. Destiny is not a matter of chance, it is a matter of choice; it is not a thing to be waited for, it is a thing to be achieved.

— William Jennings Bryan

Self-confidence is the primal source of your success; it can ultimately be more important than anything else you bring to bear on an issue. Whatever you're doing, act as if you cannot fail — and you'll be amazed by the results you get.

— Author Unknown

# It's a Wonderful Life

Sometimes it can be easy
to forget how wonderful
this life is.
Whenever that happens,
stop for a moment,
open your eyes,
and listen to your heart.
Life is filled with miracles
both big and small,
and they are all around us,
just waiting to be noticed.
It can be so easy to get caught up
in work, responsibilities, and worries,
but that's not what life is truly about.
It's about pushing beyond
the ordinary and everyday,
and finding the strength
to reach out for those dreams
in your heart.
It's about looking for the positive
even when the negative seems
overwhelming.

*You are a special person*
*who deserves all the happiness*
*the world has to offer.*
*Don't wait for something*
*huge to happen*
*to make you stop and realize*
*how wonderful this life is.*
*Open your eyes,*
*open your heart,*
*and look for a little miracle*
*in every day.*
*Reach out for your dreams,*
*stay positive,*
*and make your life*
*the wonderful success story*
*it was meant to be.*

— Rachyl Taylor

# Beginning Today…

You have a chance to be as happy as any one person has ever been. You have an opportunity to be as proud as anyone you've ever known. You have the potential to make a very special dream come true.

And all you have to do...
　　　　　　is recognize the possibilities,
the power, and the wonder of... today.

Yesterday is over and done... so let's take that out of the equation. And tomorrow isn't here yet. Whatever it may bring is surrounded by more speculation than anything, so let's take that out of the equation, too. Then do the math: what we're left with... is the perfectly exquisite gift of... today. It's right here, right now, and it hopes and prays we will do the right thing by recognizing it for the golden opportunity... and the gift... that it is.

Living life a day at a time means living a life that is blessed with awareness, appreciation, and accomplishment.

*For one day, you can be everything you were meant to be.*

*For one amazing day...*

*The weight is lifted. The path is clearer. The goal is attainable. The prayer is heard. The strength is sure. The courage is complete. The belief is steady and sweet and true.*

*For one remarkable day...*

*There is a brighter light in your life. The will to walk up the mountain takes you exactly where you want to go. The heart understands what serenity really means. And your hopes and wishes and dreams will not disappear from view.*

*For one magnificent day...*

*You can live with an abundance of love and goodness and grace shining inside of you.*

— Douglas Pagels

# Make the Most
# of Every Opportunity

*Twenty years from now you will be more disappointed by the things you didn't do than by the ones you did do. So throw off the bowlines. Sail away from the safe harbor. Catch the trade winds in your sails. Explore. Dream. Discover.*

— Mark Twain

*The golden opportunity you are seeking is in yourself. It is not in your environment; it is not in luck or chance, or the help of others; it is in yourself alone.*

— Orison Swett Marden

*If you want to succeed in the world you must make your own opportunities as you go on. The man who waits for some seventh wave to toss him on dry land will find that the seventh wave is a long time a-coming. You can commit no greater folly than to sit by the road side until someone comes along and invites you to ride with him to wealth or influence.*

— John Bartholomew Gough

# Today Is Your Time to Shine

*A day dawns, quite like other days; in it, a single hour comes, quite like other hours; but in that day and in that hour the chance of a lifetime faces us.*

— Maltbie Babcock

*This day brings to you its share of duties, opportunities and responsibilities. The spirit in which you approach the work and activities of this new day will vitally affect the results. Go forward with large confidence and high expectation. Be alert to the fresh opportunities of this day and do everything possible to advance your highest and best interests. Stimulate your mind with clear, strong, uplifting ideas of what you wish to accomplish. Realize the immense powers and resources at your personal command. Make this day mark a distinct and important advance in your progress toward a great life ideal.*

— Grenville Kleiser

More than anything else, how you manage negative elements in your life today will determine how quickly you achieve a more positive long-term outlook. If you can change your perspective, you can and will transform your life for the better.

# How to Get Through a Difficult Day

Just give things a little time.
And in the meantime...
keep believing in yourself;
take the best of care;
try to put things in perspective;
remember what's most important;
don't forget that someone cares;
search for the positive side;
learn the lessons to be learned;
and find your way through to
the inner qualities...
the strength, the smiles,
the wisdom, and the
optimistic outlook
that are such special parts
of you.

— Barin Taylor

# Difficult People

The people whom you find most difficult to deal with can also be your most valuable teachers. For your problems with them are not really due to how they are, but rather to how you respond to how they are.

Learn to deal successfully with difficult people, and you learn valuable lessons about yourself. Work to relate positively to difficult people and you develop skills that can serve you well in many other challenging situations.

People are the way they are. Get past the need to try to change them, past the need to judge or condemn, and look for the value they offer. Sometimes that value is deeply hidden, and when you find it you've found a real treasure, something few people take the time to uncover. In every difficult person you encounter, make a point to look past the difficult part and focus your attention on the person part.

The other people with whom you interact are mirrors that help you to see things within yourself. With some people, that mirror can be difficult to view, yet when you have the courage to do so, the rewards can be many and great.

— Ralph Marston

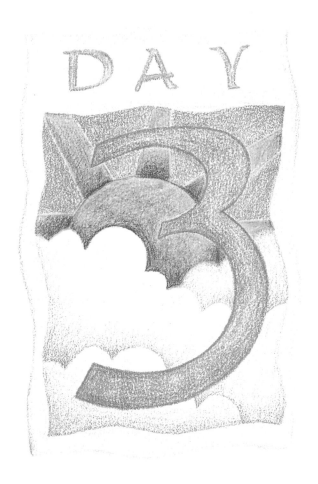

# "When the Past Intrudes..."

*Why should we be discouraged by the past? Every day is a new incarnation. It places us in different relations to all persons and events. The planet on which we live has moved steadily while we slept. It has wholly changed its orbital point... and every life meanwhile has built for itself new cells. We begin anew. We live in today. Our opportunities were never better than they are. We will not weary ourselves with regrets. We will make with every fresh day as it dawns a new declaration of independence.*

Charles B. Newcomb

It's not just today's obstructions and difficult people that hinder your progress toward a more positive outlook; your past plays a powerful role, too. Thought and habit patterns formed over the course of months or years have their own way of intruding on the present moment and affecting your moods and attitudes.

Roads not traveled, lost opportunities, and mistakes lie scattered across everyone's yesterdays; so do achievements, lessons learned, cherished memories, and untapped talents. It seems like human nature to dwell on past regrets, but you're just as capable of focusing on all the good things that have come your way and using them for inspiration.

While none of us has the power to alter the past, it is possible to shape our future. Today, you can concentrate your energies on the present, which is under your control, and let go of anything you feel is holding you back. Accept your past for what it is — the good as well as the bad — and resolve to use what you can as a steppingstone to a brighter tomorrow.

# Learn to Let Go
# of the Things
# You Can't Change

There are various ways to let go
    of something
and attitude has everything
    to do with it.
You can put it behind you,
    distance yourself from it,
accept it, learn from it,
or change your attitude
and feelings to make the best of it.
The important thing is to refuse
to let it steal any of the happiness
you are entitled to each and every day.
Purposely look at your blessings.
Listen to uplifting music,
seek out people and activities you enjoy,
and do something nice for someone.
Your future has wonderful moments
    to experience,
fun things to do,
and great people to be with.
The important thing is to transform
    the regrets of yesterday
into the joys of today.

— Barbara Cage

# Stay Focused on Today

Letting go means just what it says. It's an invitation to cease clinging to anything — whether it be an idea, a thing, an event, a particular time, or view, or desire. It is a conscious decision to release with full acceptance into the stream of present moments as they are unfolding... It's akin to letting your palm open to unhand something you have been holding on to.

— Jon Kabat-Zinn

Today is, for all that we know, the opportunity and occasion of our lives. On what we do or say today may depend the success and completeness of our entire life-struggle. It is for us, therefore, to use every moment of today as if our very eternity were dependent on its words and deeds.

— Henry Clay Trumbull

Finish every day and be done with it. You have done what you could. Some blunders and absurdities no doubt have crept in; forget them as soon as you can. Tomorrow is a new day; begin it well and serenely and with too high a spirit to be cumbered with your old nonsense. This day is all that is good and fair. It is too dear, with its hopes and invitations, to waste a moment on yesterdays.

— Ralph Waldo Emerson

# It's Never Too Late to Have a Wonderful Life

If you want to,
   you can make a change.
If it matters enough,
   you can do what it takes.
If you reach down deep enough,
   you will discover strength
   you never even knew you had.
If you reach up high enough,
   you will see the wisdom
   within your dreams.

If you reach out far enough,
   you will find a helping hand;
   one that will help you
   understand that if you stay
   strong and don't give up on
   your dreams, your dreams
   won't give up on you.

And if you need a reminder
of how great it will be
to make a change and give
yourself the gift of living
in the middle of
a new beginning...

just keep on striving
for your goal.

And pretty soon,
you'll see...
you're going to be
smiling every step
of the way...

on the way to a
wonderful life.

— Douglas Pagels

# The Power of Positive Change

*Our destiny changes with our thought; we shall become what we wish to become, do what we wish to do, when our habitual thought corresponds with our desire.*

— Orison Swett Marden

*The important thing is this: To be able at any moment to sacrifice what we are for what we could become.*

— Charles du Bois

*Start where you stand and never mind the past,*
*The past won't help you in beginning new,*
*If you have left it all behind at last*
*Why, that's enough, you're done with it, you're through;*
*This is another chapter in the book,*
*This is another race that you have planned,*
*Don't give the vanished days a backward look,*
*Start where you stand.*

— Berton Braley

# Always Expect the Best

*Always expect the best. Then if you have to hurdle a few tough problems, you will have generated the strength and courage to do so. Successful businesses are forever planning and dreaming ahead. And so should we, as individuals... We must be constructive in our thoughts and our attitude toward life.*

— George Matthew Adams

*Becoming familiar with optimism, reflecting on it, and making it a priority to become more optimistic are powerful life tools. Seeing optimism as a possibility, instead of dismissing it as a sign of naïveté, gives you more options. It allows you to know that very often you have a clear choice about how to respond to or think about something in your life. Optimism is an attitude or outlook about something, and as such it nudges your perception one way or the other. Consciously choosing optimism over pessimism can sometimes make the difference between success and failure, winning and losing, being neutral and getting depressed, moving forward or giving up.*

— Richard Carlson

# If You Want to Feel Optimistic Every Day...

*Start each morning with a smile on your face. Keep wearing that smile as you go about your work, and you'll make that day an optimistic one. Treat each person you meet like a VIP. Take an enthusiastic interest in them by asking questions and listening closely. Find out what their passions are. Remember your good manners and exercise them often. Say "please" and "thank you."*

*Find joy on the job. Take a task and make it fun. Be the cheerleader of your work team. Count your blessings — in a waiting room, in your journal, or in your car while you're stuck in traffic.*

*Take a vacation. You don't have to travel to an exotic island. Just go to a quiet room where you can relax with your peaceful thoughts. Breathe in all the peace and feel the calmness quieting your mind and refreshing your spirits.*

*Take opportunities to learn new skills, have new adventures, and make new friends. If you want to go places, you have to grow. If you want to enjoy the spice of life, you have to cultivate a variety of people.*

*Stay healthy — mentally, physically, and spiritually. Read. Ride a bike. Take walks. Lift weights. Talk every day to your Higher Power, and listen to the message you receive of love, comfort, and healing peace.*

*Be proud of who you are. Walk tall. Let all your actions reflect the good person you are. Let the words you speak honor all your beauty and wonder. Remember to begin each day in the light of love from all those whose lives you touch so beautifully.*

— Jacqueline Schiff

# The Benefits of Failure

"Failure" is a relative term. What you learn from life's setbacks and how you move on afterwards is more important in the long run than the specific details of any particular reversal. Look at failure in a positive way as a learning experience that makes you stronger and better prepared to overcome similar challenges in the future.

*The only real mistake we make is the one from which we learn nothing.*

— John Wesley Powell

*Our achievements speak for themselves. What we have to keep track of are our failures, discouragements, and doubts. We tend to forget the past difficulties, the many false starts, and the painful groping. We see our past achievements as the end result of a clean forward thrust, and our present difficulties as signs of decline and decay.*

— Eric Hoffer

*It is a mistake to suppose that men succeed through success; they much oftener succeed through failures. Precept, study, advice, and example could never have taught them so well as failure has done.*

— Samuel Smiles

# The Past Is Past, but Tomorrow Will Last Forever

*Our lives have so many*
*backward glances in them,*
*don't they...*
*Thinking back to how things*
*were and how things might*
*have been...*

*There's nothing wrong with*
*thinking back; but it probably is*
*a mistake to dwell on*
*    the past "what ifs."*
*Instead, we should concentrate*
*on today, on tomorrow,*
*and on the tomorrows yet to be.*

*There are a lot of beautiful days*
*    yet to come.*

*The past is past...*
*    but tomorrow will last forever.*
*Let each tomorrow*
*fill your heart with love*
*    and laughter,*
*your days with dreams come true,*
*    and your life with so much*
*        happiness to look forward to.*

— Laurel Atherton

# "Check Your Progress!"

*We are either progressing or retrograding all the while;*
*there is no such thing as remaining stationary in this life.*

James Freeman Clarke

Today you're halfway through on your way to a more optimistic attitude. This is a great opportunity to evaluate how you're doing — even if you're not as far along as you hoped or planned to be. At this stage, it's important to remind yourself that any and all progress is a positive advance in the right direction. Over time, little steps add up into great life-altering changes.

Procrastination and loss of momentum rank high on the list of potential roadblocks that can stall your progress. Two of your most powerful tools to counteract these forces are *patience* and *perseverance*. They enable you to continue on even when the daily frustrations make you feel like quitting or falling back on your old beliefs and behavior patterns. They give you the strength to make changes and the faith that your life is unfolding perfectly.

All progress is relative; we each arrive at our destinations in different ways and at our own pace. Set your own personal benchmarks for measuring your journey and do your best to meet them — but don't beat yourself up if you fall behind. Keep in mind that while it's important to get where you're going, there are a lot of beautiful things to see and do and experience along the way. Be patient, persevere... and someday you'll be exactly where you dream about today.

If you're not as far along as you thought you would be... don't worry!

Patience and perseverance have a magical effect before which difficulties disappear and obstacles vanish.

— John Quincy Adams

Nothing in the world can take the place of persistence. Talent will not; nothing is more common than unsuccessful men with talent. Genius will not; unrewarded genius is almost a proverb. Education will not; the world is full of educated failures. Persistence and determination alone are omnipotent.

— Calvin Coolidge

Have patience with all things, but chiefly have patience with yourself. Do not lose courage in considering your own imperfections, but instantly set about remedying them — every day begin the task anew.

— St. Francis de Sales

# Keep Everything in Perspective

$S$ome of us will experience waves of glory and success, while others will know the impact of disaster. Everyone has their day when they can do no wrong. And everyone suffers defeat sometimes, but life wouldn't be exciting if there were no challenges nor would there be any reason to focus or anything to learn. A perfect world in which defeat did not exist would not be perfect at all.

— Milton Willis and Michael Willis

$N$o one moves upward in a path of unbroken progress to the attainment of perfection. What happens is that — if we are working rightly — we move upward, but with a series of "downs" as well as "ups." We move steadily forward for a while, and then we have a little setback. Then we move forward again, and presently we have another little setback of some kind, and so forth. These setbacks are not important as long as the general movement of our lives is upward.

— Emmet Fox

# What Is Your Attitude?

Your life depends most of all upon your attitude toward life. If life seems purposeless and meaningless, it will be so. If it glows with purpose and challenge you'll be inspired to make the most of it.

Your attitude toward people determines your relations with them. If you have an attitude of faith, understanding, good will, and love, people will respond. If you expect to find the good in people, you will find it.

Your attitude toward your life work will determine your contribution to your time. Not what you can get but what you can give is the mark of greatness.

Your attitude toward things of the spirit will narrow or expand your life. Emphasis on material things limits and restricts. Recognition of the power of the spirit enriches, enlarges, and ennobles.

*Your attitude is an expression of your standard of values, your ideals, your philosophy of life. Your attitude becomes a deep subconscious habit pattern. It is the fundamental way you respond to life in your moment-by-moment living.*

*Attitude is not what you are now and then. It is the way you think, feel, and act, day after day. It is the basic design of your life.*

*Creative attitude is a supreme personal effort to maintain, amidst the vicissitudes of life, a level of thinking that will help you to be the person you want to be.*

*Your attitude is **you**. Emerson said it well: "A man is what he thinks about all day."*

— Wilferd A. Peterson

# How to Maintain (or Regain) Your Momentum

*Go forward with your shoulders back, your head high, and with a smile. With your enthusiastic spirit, perseverance, and integrity of character, put your intelligence, talents, and passion into action.*

— Jacqueline Schiff

*If you've lost focus, just sit down and be still.*
*Take the idea and rock it to and fro.*
*Keep some of it and throw some away, and*
*it will renew itself. You need do no more.*

— Clarissa Pinkola Estés

*Every now and then go away, have a little relaxation, for when you come back to your work your judgment will be surer. Go some distance away because then the work appears smaller and more of it can be taken in at a glance and a lack of harmony and proportion is more readily seen.*

— Leonardo da Vinci

# Take Mini Vacations

The demands of life often require that we stand back and look at our life from the outside-in. This approach gives us a new perspective or clearer view or understanding of what is really going on. It is like watching yourself in action.

When we do this, we begin to realize the patterns and life dramas we create. People who are happy tend to be realistic in their view of life and themselves. They seldom are out of touch with the realities of their existence. This does not mean that these people have it "all together all the time," they just see through the illusions and stuff of life better.

One of the best ways to accomplish this is to take some time off and get away from the normal issues, pressures, and routines in life. By taking a mini vacation or retreat for two to three days, you change your environment and routines. This alone can be therapeutic and revitalizing.

During these little trips, and it doesn't matter where they are — the mountains, beach, or any location that gives you a change of scenery — you can spend time thinking, relaxing, meditating, reviewing your life, or just having fun. The point of the diversion is to give you the opportunity to look at your life with a different perspective. This can keep you on track toward the life you were meant to live.

— Tim Connor

# Overcome Procrastination...

The first principle is: break it down.
No matter what you're trying to accomplish, whether it's writing
a book, climbing a mountain, or painting a house, the key to
achievement is your ability to break down the task into
manageable pieces and knock them off one at one time. Focus
on accomplishing what's right in front of you at this moment.
Ignore what's off in the distance someplace. Substitute real-time
positive thinking for negative future visualization. That's the first
all-important technique for bringing an end to procrastination.

— Jim Rohn

Know the true value of time; snatch, seize, and
enjoy every moment of it. No idleness, no delay, no
procrastination; never put off till tomorrow what
you can do today.

— Earl of Chesterfield

We shall never have more time. We have, and have always
had, all the time there is. No object is served in waiting until
next week or even until tomorrow. Keep going day in and day
out. Concentrate on something useful. Having decided to
achieve a task, achieve it at all costs.

— Arnold Bennett

*I*dentify where your procrastination starts. Do you bog down at the **stage of inception** before you begin? Do you snare yourself at the **planning stage**, when you first start to think about designing your approach? Do you set up your plans and organizing scheme then **fizzle in following through**? Do you start quickly then **fade in the stretch**? Do you finish what you start but fail to capitalize on your accomplishment by **going the extra mile**?

— William J. Knaus


*C*ommitment and determination are powerful tools that can overcome even the worst tendencies to procrastinate. Today, take a project you've been putting off and do something positive about it. If you can only spend five minutes on it, commit yourself completely for that amount of time and put forth your best effort. At the end of your allotted time, set the project aside. Repeat this for the next few days, and in a week you may be surprised at the progress you can make in a relatively short amount of time. Take each step with courage and faith, knowing you have what it takes to complete the journey.

— Jon Peyton

# Measure Progress in Your Own Way

It's easy to get discouraged when you compare yourself to those who seem to have gone so much farther down the road you're traveling. Remember that we're each on our own individual journey to a unique destiny — not competing in a race to see who arrives first. So measure progress by your own milestones. Keep your spirits upbeat and your heart full of hope — because you're on your way to a beautiful destination.

*Don't judge each day by the harvest you reap, but by the seeds you plant.*

— Robert Louis Stevenson

*I count that day as wisely spent in which I do some good for someone who is far away... or shares my neighborhood. A day devoted to the deed that lends a helping hand and demonstrates a willingness to care and understand. I long to be of usefulness in little ways and large, without a selfish motive and without the slightest charge — because in my philosophy there never is a doubt that all of us here on earth must help each other out. I feel that day is fruitful, and the time is worth the while, when I promote the happiness of one enduring smile.*

— Author Unknown

# What Did You Do Today?

Is anybody happier because you passed this way?
Does anyone remember that you spoke today?
The day is almost over, and its toiling time is through:
Is there anyone to utter now a kindly word of you?
Can you say tonight in parting with the day that's slipping fast,
That you helped a single person of the many that you passed?
Is a single heart rejoicing over what you did or said?
Does the one whose hopes were fading now with courage look ahead?
Did you waste the day or use it? Was it well or sorely spent?
Did you leave a trail of kindness, or a scar of discontent?
As you close your eyes in slumber, do you think that you can say:
You have earned one more tomorrow by what you did today?

— Author Unknown

A day is well lived in which you have
put a fine resolution into practice, achieved
a definite purpose, done some worthy act of kindness,
or rendered a noble service to others. True service
is not limited to time or place. Today is the day
to do something fine and noble.

— Grenville Kleiser

# "Remember You Are Not Alone..."

*Associating with positive-thinking people can make a world of difference in how you see things... Picking and choosing our friends and associates wisely is a very important step in cultivating optimism. But the best part is that if you are a positive person you are more likely to attract positive people who can be a wonderful influence in your life.*

Mary Lou Retton

Your talents, experience, and knowledge are powerful tools you can use to create a positive mindset. But one of the greatest assets you will ever have are the people in your life who believe in you. We all need others to turn to for feedback, advice, and encouragement. Surround yourself with people who radiate confidence, passion, and commitment to their own goals, and let them inspire you.

You can also discover a lot from those who have come before you. History is full of people who have already achieved the exact same kinds of goals you're dreaming about. A lot of them have written books or had books written about their accomplishments. Benefit from their experiences, and you will save yourself years of trial and error. If you faithfully duplicate their steps and adapt them to your own circumstances, you should receive much the same results.

Ultimately, the greatest achievements in our lives come about as the result of teamwork. With the right group of people, there are no limits to what you can strive for; you can literally change the world in positive and profound ways.

# Build a Strong
# Support Group

*K*eep away from people who try to belittle your ambitions. Small people always do that, but the really great make you feel that you, too, can become great.

— Mark Twain

*Y*ou can make more friends in two months by becoming interested in other people than you can in two years by trying to get other people interested in you.

— Dale Carnegie

*B*uild a group of two or more like-minded people to meet with regularly who believe in you and can affirm you. Discuss your dream with them. Let them help you clarify your dream on paper and remind you to stay on course. The people with whom you associate can have a dramatic effect on your life... when you gravitate toward those who believe in your potential, you cannot help but grow.

— Mary Manin Morrissey

# Learn All You Can from Those Who Have Already Succeeded

No one lives long enough to learn everything they need to learn starting from scratch. To be successful, we absolutely, positively have to find people who have already paid the price to learn the things that we need to learn to achieve our goals.

— Brian Tracy

To profit from good advice requires more wisdom than to give it.

— John Churton Collins

A hundred times every day I remind myself that my inner and outer life depend on the labors of other men, living and dead, and that I must exert myself in order to give in the same measure as I have received and am still receiving.

— Albert Einstein

# "Trust Others, and They Will Be True to You"

Trust is the foundation of any human relationship. With it, anything is possible.

Trust between two people is displayed in many different ways. Most of all, it means never having to wonder if what you're being told is true. It's knowing that what you see and hear from another person is real and sincere.

It's feeling safe and comfortable whenever you're together. It means being able to share anything and know it will be held in the strictest confidence.

It's knowing that you would do anything for each other and expect nothing in return. It means that your relationship will always be secure enough to grow.

*Trust is feeling confident that whenever you're apart you'll always behave as if you were together.*

*It's caring how the other person feels and respecting their needs and opinions. It's being there for each other while sharing both the good and difficult times together.*

*It means never having to worry or think your relationship is anything but what you've honestly shared with each other.*

*With trust between two people, anything is possible.*

— Tim Tweedie

# The Amazing Power of Teamwork

However you can, discover those people in the world with whom you share common values and attitudes. Join together with them and do all you can to encourage, assist, and inspire each other in the pursuit of your individual goals and objectives. In the company of these fellow travelers, you will expand your horizons as you explore new ways of thinking and being in this world. Above all, what you achieve as a thriving member of this group will far surpass anything you could imagine on your own.

— Cole Washington

It is one of the beautiful compensations of this life that no one can sincerely try to help another without helping himself.

— Charles Dudley Warner

Cooperation between members of a team — forged in the arena of competition found in every field of endeavor — supercharges the evolution of each individual's abilities. Cooperation enables them to transform themselves in ways that might otherwise be impossible.

— Mitchell Lawes

# 11 Commandments for an Enthusiastic Team

1. Help each other be right... not wrong.

2. Look for ways to make new ideas work...
   not for reasons they won't.

3. If in doubt... check it out! Don't make negative
   assumptions about each other.

4. Help each other win and take pride in each
   other's victories.

5. Speak positively about each other and about
   your organization at every opportunity.

6. Maintain a positive mental attitude no matter
   what the circumstances.

7. Act with initiative and courage as if it all
   depends on you.

8. Do everything with enthusiasm...
   it's contagious.

9. Whatever you want... give it away.

10. Don't lose faith... never give up.

11. Have fun!

— Ian Percy

# You'll Receive Great Rewards
# When You Give to Others

*Giving is one of the nicest ways
to let others know how we feel,
and a wonderful way to express
    our true nature.
We can give a smile, a hug,
kind words of praise,
encouragement, or compliments.
It's not the value of what we
    give away,
but the thoughtfulness of being
someone who is willing to give
    and actually does it.*

*There are thousands of opportunities
    for each of us to be generous,
and it's caring, generous people
who make this world a better place.
And anyone who is on
    the receiving end
of someone's generosity
knows how beautiful
    the thoughts and feelings are
behind the act of giving.*

— Dena Dilaconi

It costs so little, I wonder why
We give it so little thought;
A smile, kind words, a glance, a touch —
What magic by them is wrought.

— Author Unknown

All of us can give friendship to those who need it; loyalty to those who depend upon us; courtesy to all those with whom we come in contact; kindness to those whose paths may cross ours; understanding to those whose views may not be exactly in accord with our opinions.

— Carl E. Holmes

You will find, as you look back on your life, that the moments that stand out are the moments when you have done things for others.

— Henry Drummond

# Share Your Optimistic Spirit with the World

*Treat people as if they were what they ought to be and you help them to become what they are capable of being.*

— Johann Wolfgang von Goethe

*The generous heart is the happy heart. If you have beautiful thoughts, why should you hoard them? If you have wonderful gifts, why should you hide them? If you have a warm, loving hand, why should you close it against your breast instead of opening it in cordial greeting to your brother man? One little act of generosity is a small thing, yet you cannot perform the most trivial task which will be a blessing to someone else without being benefited by it yourself. Someone has said, "Charity is never lost; it may meet with ingratitude, or be of no service to those on whom it was bestowed, yet it ever does a work of beauty and grace upon the heart of the giver."*

— Ida Scott Taylor

It's what each of us sows, and how, that gives to us character and prestige. Seeds of kindness, goodwill, and human understanding, planted in fertile soil, spring up into deathless friendships, big deeds of worth, and a memory that will not soon fade.

— George Matthew Adams

As you reach forward with one hand, accept the advice of those who have gone before you, and in the same manner reach back with the other hand to those who follow you; for life is a fragile chain of experiences held together by love. Take pride in being a strong link in that chain. Discipline yourself, but do not be harsh. The pleasures of life are yours to be taken. Share them with others, but always remember that you, too, have earned the right to partake.

— Tim Murtaugh

The best portion of a good man's life is his little, nameless, unremembered acts of kindness and love.

— William Wordsworth

# "Appreciate the Little Blessings..."

*I will greet this day with love in my heart. And how will I do this?*
*Henceforth will I look on all things with love and I will be born again.*
*I will love the sun for it warms my bones; yet I will love the rain for it*
*cleanses my spirit. I will love the light for it shows me the way; yet I will*
*love the darkness for it shows me the stars. I will welcome happiness*
*for it enlarges my heart; yet I will endure sadness for it opens my soul.*
*I will acknowledge rewards for they are my due; yet I will welcome*
*obstacles for they are my challenge.*

Og Mandino

One of the greatest secrets to achieving and maintaining a positive attitude is also a simple one: Learn to appreciate what you already have. It's okay to dream about all the things you want to see and do and be... but it's just as important to look around you and realize how blessed you really are in this moment. Health, relationships, the beauty of the world around you — these are the greatest gifts of life, though so often they are taken for granted.

Today, you might try taking some time to make a list of what you're most thankful for. It doesn't have to be just about the big obvious things; it's even more instructive to focus on those little blessings tucked away like sweet surprises throughout your day. No matter how small it might seem to someone else, include it on your list if it's important to you.

When you see your blessings with new eyes and a renewed sense of gratitude, you're attuned to receive even greater gifts from life.

# Things to Be Thankful For

*Freedom and honesty...*
> to truly get to know yourself and what you want in life.

*Joy and wonder...*
> the kind you get from loving someone more deeply
> than you ever dreamed possible, and the happiness of
> sharing life with them.

*Strength and confidence...*
> the kind that comes from those experiences that teach
> you that you can rely on yourself and you do have
> something to say about your destiny.

*Courage and energy...*
> to pursue the adventure of exploring your own dreams —
> big or small.

*Tolerance, insight, and perspective...*
> to see others as they are and let them be, along with
> the gentle openness to learn from them and apply
> what you can to your own life, while still maintaining
> the values that are right for you.

*Peace and happiness...*
> the kind that comes from knowing you are loved.

— Deeva D. Boleman

# Cultivate an Attitude of Gratitude

*Cherish your visions; cherish your ideals;
cherish the music that stirs in your heart,
the beauty that forms in your mind, the
loveliness that drapes your purest thoughts,
for out of them will grow delightful
conditions, all heavenly environment; of these
if you but remain true to them, your world
will at last be built...*

— James Allen

*Our real blessings often appear to us in the shape of pains,
losses, and disappointments; but let us have patience, and we
soon shall see them in their proper figures.*

— Joseph Addison

*If you want to live more you must master the art
of appreciating the little, everyday blessings of life.
This is not altogether a golden world, but there are
countless gleams of gold to be discovered in it if
we give our minds to them.*

— Henry Alford Porter

# You Deserve to Be Happy!
## ...Here's How You Can Be

Happiness is a state of mind, an inner peace, and a restful soul. You cannot buy it at a store, order it online, or find it in your favorite catalog. You can't get promoted into happiness or graduate into it (even if you are at the head of your class). You won't find it at a party or in a bar — it won't be in the car you drive or the clothes you wear.

Happiness is the acceptance of what life has to offer, and the desire to grab all that is within your reach. It also means being able to let go of what you cannot have, with no regrets — because all the things we desire are not necessarily achievable. Even if they were, they alone would not bring us true happiness.

*Happiness is the place you're at right now... once you learn to open your heart. We can all appreciate what we do have. We can all be proud of our achievements, which are as infinite as the stars if you know how to count them. We can all be pleased with what we are each designed to be — an individual like no one else before.*

*So open your heart, set your inhibitions free, and receive your happiness. You are blessed with it, and you deserve to experience it.*

— Karen M. Talmo

# You Have a Lot to Feel Positive About

*Every morning, you're given a brand-new opportunity to fulfill your hopes and dreams — and this day may bring you happiness in ways you have never experienced before.*

*You have people in your life who care about you; they are worth more than anything else in this world.*

*You have all the seasons and the beauty they bring to your life: the hopeful springs, the blossoming summers, the brilliant autumns, and the quiet fire of winter days.*

*You have work that fills your hands with skills and your mind with learning; remember that you can find the potential for satisfaction in every job you do.*

*In the end... if you can find a way to feel positive every day for just about everything in your life — you'll gain a happiness that only the wisest among us ever know.*

— Jon Peyton

# Find Fulfillment in
# Life's Simple Joys

To find the universal elements enough; to find the air and
the water exhilarating; to be refreshed by a morning walk
or an evening saunter; to be thrilled by the stars at night;
to be elated over a bird's nest or a wildflower in spring —
these are some of the rewards of the simple life.

— John Burroughs

Most of the luxuries, and many of the
so-called comforts of life, are not only not
indispensable, but positive hindrances to the
elevation of mankind. With respect to luxuries
and comforts, the wisest have even lived a
more simple and meager life than the poor.

— Henry David Thoreau

The best things in life are nearest: Breath in your nostrils, light
in your eyes, flowers at your feet, duties at your hand, the path
of right just before you. Then do not grasp at the stars, but do
life's plain, common work as it comes, certain that daily duties
and daily bread are the sweetest things in life.

— Robert Louis Stevenson

# "You Really Are on Your Way!"

*Every day you may make progress. Every step may be fruitful.*
*Yet there will stretch out before you an ever-lengthening, ever-ascending,*
*ever-improving path. You know you will never get to the end*
*of the journey. But this, so far from discouraging, only adds to*
*the joy and glory of the climb.*

Sir Winston Churchill

Here it is already — the end of the week! One way or another, you made it through. Look back over the days just past and celebrate any steps you took toward achieving the goals you wrote about that first day. Assess your progress, but be sure to take some time for relaxation and fun, too. Treat yourself like the special person you are.

Hopefully this book has given you some ideas about planning your journey, along with a little motivation to get you further along your chosen path. This really is only the beginning of the beautiful voyage you're making to a better, brighter future — for yourself, your friends and loved ones, and a world in need of the most optimistic people it can find. The road you're on will take a lifetime to unfold; remember the real reward is not your final destination, but the wonderful experiences you'll have along the way.

Today and in all the weeks ahead... be one of those rare people in this world who enjoys life to the fullest every day. Be optimistic about your future, realistic about your past, and an inspiration to everyone you meet. Be the winner you were born to be!

# Today, Treat Yourself like the Special Person You Are

If you do one thing today, it should be to
Treat yourself like a special person.

Make a little time in your day just for you.
Buy yourself something you really like.
Praise yourself much more often.

If you do these things,
You will smile at everyone you meet,
Happiness will shine from your eyes,
And the world will smile with you.

So today, treat yourself like a special person
Because
You are one.

— Maria Mullins

# Relax, Renew, Recharge – Have Fun!

*Now and then it's good to pause in our pursuit of happiness and just be happy.*

— Guillaume Apollinaire

While it's essential to pursue your dreams with all the enthusiasm, determination, and dedication you can muster, it's equally important to balance your work with opportunities for rest and relaxation.

Be sure to take one day a week — like today — and give yourself a break from the world. Spend at least a little time doing something you enjoy — whether it's spending time with family and friends or going off into your own solitude; working in the yard or taking a nap; reading a book or going for a bike ride or a hike.

Ultimately, relaxation and having fun are as important as any other ingredients in creating and maintaining a positive attitude. You'll benefit from it in more ways than you can imagine, and not always in ways you can see. Sometimes you have to step away from what you're focusing on in order to see it more clearly. Giving yourself some time off actually makes you more open to fresh insights and ideas. You may even discover a dream or new direction that changes your world forever.

# You Can Go Wherever You Want to Go

Live in the present, but be conscious and concerned
about all that tomorrow may have in store for you.
Prepare for unexpected challenges and demands,
realizing life will always be full of changes.
Give all that you have toward all the things that you want.
In essence, life is about making dreams come true,
making the things that you believe in reality.
You alone must find your way through time.
Life is everyone's personal responsibility to manage and create.
Family and friends will be there to help us
but the bottom line is... we are accountable to ourselves.
We should not expect others to constantly guide us
through each and every twist and turn in the road.

So if you are traveling by car, fill it up with gas
and keep your eyes open to the roads ahead of you.
If you are traveling by foot, wear comfortable shoes
that fit your feet, and keep your laces tied tight.
And if you are one of the few who travel
in the winds and through the skies,
open your wings wide
and remember to gaze out in all directions.
Feel thankful for the privilege of being who you are
with the talents that you have
and the freedom to choose wherever you want to go.

— Deanna Beisser

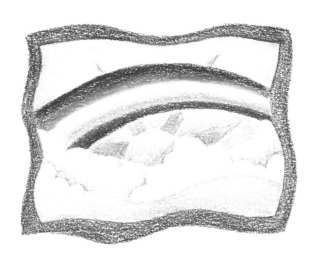

# "Every Day
# You Are on the Way"

Each and every day, you are on the way
to becoming the person you were meant
to be. Every day brings you closer to reaching
your potential, your hopes, and your wishes
on a thousand stars. Each day gives you a new
opportunity to be the miracle that you are.

You are wished all the wonders you seek.

You are given the chance to put yesterday
behind you, and to keep only the lessons
you may have learned from the past. You
are provided with all the possibilities that
can possibly come to this one day... and
to find a way to honor all those things
you want to last forever and ever.

*Make yourself so proud! Make choices that are compassionate and loving and right. Learn the power of saying "no" to the wrong things and "yes!" to a more beautiful life.*

*Remember: A life well lived is simply a compilation of days well spent. So treasure the tremendous value of the moments right before your eyes. Reach out for the prizes you seek, and get a little closer to them with the setting of every sun.*

*Make **this one day** a journey of love and achievement, gently powered by all the benefits of understanding, commitment, and hope. Be healthy, happy, and continually rewarded for doing things that you know in your heart... are right.*

*May you discover every joy that wants to come true for you... on your precious journey through life.*

— Douglas Pagels

# ACKNOWLEDGMENTS

We gratefully acknowledge the permission granted by the following authors, publishers, and authors' representatives to reprint poems or excerpts from their publications.

Tanya P. Shubin for "In the Week Ahead... Be the Person You Are Meant to Be." Copyright © 2004 by Tanya P. Shubin. All rights reserved.

Dan Custer for "Every morning is a fresh beginning...." Copyright © by Dan Custer. All rights reserved.

Prentice-Hall, Inc., for "The positive thinker has a longer..." from POSITIVE THINKING FOR A TIME LIKE THIS by Norman Vincent Peale. Copyright © 1961, 1975 by Prentice-Hall, Inc. All rights reserved.

Thomas Nelson, Inc., Nashville, TN, for "As you begin changing your thinking..." from DEVELOPING THE LEADER WITHIN YOU by John C. Maxwell. Copyright © 1993 by Injoy, Inc. All rights reserved.

Hay House, Inc., for "You can increase your feeling..." from CONFIDENCE: FINDING IT AND LIVING IT by Barbara De Angelis. Copyright © 1995 by Barbara De Angelis. All rights reserved.

The Daily Motivator for "Difficult People" from "Your Job Today" by Ralph Marston. Copyright © 2003 by Ralph S. Marston, Jr. All rights reserved.

Barbara Cage for "Learn to Let Go of the Things You Can't Change." Copyright © 2004 by Barbara Cage. All rights reserved.

Hyperion for "Letting go means just what it says" from WHEREVER YOU GO, THERE YOU ARE by Jon Kabat-Zinn. Copyright © 1994 by Jon Kabat-Zinn. All rights reserved. And for "Becoming familiar with optimism..." from WHAT ABOUT THE BIG STUFF? by Richard Carlson. Copyright © 2002 by Richard Carlson, Ph.D. Reprinted by permission of Hyperion. All rights reserved.

Jacqueline Schiff for "Start each morning with a smile...." Copyright © 2004 by Jacqueline Schiff. All rights reserved.

Lillian Fabilli Osborne for "Our achievements speak for themselves," from REFLECTIONS ON THE HUMAN CONDITION by Eric Hoffer, published by HarperCollins Publishers. Copyright © 1973 by Eric Hoffer. All rights reserved.

HarperCollins Publishers for "No one moves upward..." from MAKE YOUR LIFE WORTH WHILE by Emmet Fox. Copyright 1942, 1943, 1944, 1945, 1946 by Emmet Fox. All rights reserved.

Milton Willis and Michael Willis for "Some of us will experience...." Copyright © 2004 by Milton Willis and Michael Willis. All rights reserved.

Ballantine Books, a division of Random House, Inc., for "If you've lost focus, just sit down..." from WOMEN WHO RUN WITH WOLVES by Clarissa Pinkola Estés. Copyright © 1992 by Clarissa Pinkola Estés. All rights reserved.

Executive Books for "Take mini vacations" from THE ROAD TO HAPPINESS IS FULL OF POTHOLES by Tim Connor. Copyright © 1998 by Tim Connor. All rights reserved.

The Heacock Literary Agency for "What Is Your Attitude?" from THE ART OF LIVING by Wilferd A. Peterson, published by Galahad Books. Copyright © 1960, 1961, 1962, 1963, 1966 by Wilferd A. Peterson. All rights reserved.

Jim Rohn for "The first principle is: break it down," from "Ending Procrastination." Copyright © 2001 by Jim Rohn International. All rights reserved.

John Wiley & Sons, Inc. for "Identify where your procrastination..." from DO IT NOW! by Dr. William J. Knaus. Copyright © by Dr. William J. Knaus. All rights reserved.

Broadway Books, a division of Random House, Inc., for "Associating with positive-thinking people..." from MARY LOU RETTON'S GATEWAYS TO HAPPINESS by Mary Lou Retton. Copyright © 2000 by MLR Entertainment, Inc., and Momentum Partners, Inc. All rights reserved.

Simon & Schuster Adult Publishing Group for "You can make more friends..." from HOW TO WIN FRIENDS AND INFLUENCE PEOPLE by Dale Carnegie. Copyright 1936 by Dale Carnegie, copyright renewed © 1964 by Donna Dale Carnegie and Dorothy Carnegie. All rights reserved. And for "A hundred times every day..." from LIVING PHILOSOPHIES by Albert Einstein, John Dewey, and James W. Jeans, Sr. Copyright 1931 by Simon & Schuster. All rights reserved.

Bantam Books, a division of Random House, Inc., for "Build a group of two or more like-minded people..." from BUILDING YOUR FIELD OF DREAMS by Mary Manin Morrissey. Copyright © 1996 by Mary Manin Morrissey. All rights reserved. And for "I will greet this day with love..." from THE GREATEST SECRET IN THE WORLD by Og Mandino. Copyright © 1972 by Og Mandino. All rights reserved.

Berrett-Koehler Publishers, Inc. for "No one lives long enough..." from THE 100 ABSOLUTELY UNBREAKABLE LAWS OF BUSINESS SUCCESS by Brian Tracy. Copyright © 2000 by Brian Tracy. All rights reserved. www.bkconnection.com. Reprinted with permission of the publisher.

Tim Tweedie for "Trust is the foundation of...." Copyright © 2004 by Tim Tweedie. All rights reserved.

Ian Percy for "11 Commandments for an Enthusiastic Team." Copyright © 2002 by Ian Percy Corporation. All rights reserved.

Carl E. Holmes for "All of us can give friendship...." Copyright © Carl E. Holmes. All rights reserved.

Karen M. Talmo for "You Deserve to Be Happy!" Copyright © 2004 by Karen M. Talmo. All rights reserved.

Curtis Brown Group Limited for "Every day you may make progress" from THOUGHTS AND ADVENTURES by Winston S. Churchill. Copyright © 1932 by Winston S. Churchill. All rights reserved.

Maria Mullins for "Today, Treat Yourself like the Special Person You Are." Copyright © 2004 by Maria Mullins. All rights reserved.

Deanna Beisser for "You Can Go Wherever You Want to Go." Copyright © 2004 by Deanna Beisser. All rights reserved.

A careful effort has been made to trace the ownership of selections used in this anthology in order to obtain permission to reprint copyrighted material and give proper credit to the copyright owners. If any error or omission has occurred, it is completely inadvertent, and we would like to make corrections in future editions provided that written notification is made to the publisher:

BLUE MOUNTAIN ARTS, INC., P.O. Box 4549, Boulder, Colorado 80306.